Chafing Dish Book

Chafing Dish

BOOK

by HELEN EVANS BROWN

THE WARD RITCHIE PRESS · LOS ANGELES

To Bill and Oakley

Note to Revised Edition

Since the completion of the original edition of this book in 1950, electric skillets have become very popular. Any of these recipes may be made in this versatile utensil. The electric skillet has the advantage of quick temperature adjustment, but it lacks the charm and drama of the classic chafing dish.

Introduction

THE *revived and tremendous interest in the chafing dish will indubitably produce a spate of cookery books on the subject, as it did at the turn of the century. How many such books were published at that time I do not know; I myself have twenty-two of them and there must be many more. The amazing thing about them was that they were so alike. The fact that they all contain recipes for Welsh rabbit and lobster Newberg I forgive—indeed I have to, as I include them here—but I find it difficult to overlook the fact that the rest of their recipes were so similar. To own one book was to own them all, for with few exceptions they agreed on what dishes were proper for a chafing dish. This was probably because chafing dish cookery was high style in those days, and so the social dictators, even as today, ruled what was "correct" and got away with it. In spite of the gastronomical limitations put upon the chafing dish, its use became an almost frantic enthusiasm and resulted in some ridiculous fashions.*

Thomas A. Murrey who in the eighties turned out innumerable and enchanting little cookery books, attempted to defend the chafing dish cult: "The sound common sense displayed in this fad shows that society is not the vapid thing our humorous journalists would have us believe it to be." Mr. Murrey said that chafing dish cookery had been taken up by the "amateur and professional gourmets of Gotham. Chafing dish clubs have not only been formed in the family circle, but the leading clubs of New York have taken up the subject with the cheerful prospect that in a few years from now to be an American will be synonymous with possessing a knowledge of the Art of Cookery." Poor Mr. Murrey!—his hopes were in vain, for before the century passed the chafing dish had become the emblem not of the gourmet, but of the snob. A tongue-in-cheek comment by Christine Terhune Herrick, in 1895, gives a hint of what was happening. "The most sedate householder now owns one which is often expensive enough to exonerate its proprietor from any suspicion of Bohemianism," and she continues, "When the cooking of a dinner entrée in a chafing dish is personally conducted by an irreproachable butler, the acme of elegance and incongruity has surely been reached."

The machine became more important than its product. Chafing dishes were made of every conceivable metal and in every conceivable design. One, a sea-going affair, was so contrived that no matter what angle the yacht assumed, the blazer, water jacket, and spirit lamp would all retain their upright and decorous position. Another conceit was the individual chafing dish, one of which was set before each guest at the table, not—and this might be fun—so that he could create his own concoction, but so that some kitchen-cooked morsel could be presented with éclat. Or perhaps the idea was to emulate Seneca who said of the Ancients' chafing dishes: "Daintiness gave birth to this

*invention in order that no viand should be chilled, and that
everything should be hot enough to please the pampered palate.'
Then there were the appurtenances—elaborate fuel flagons,
trays, special forks and spoons and condiment casters were considered essential. Some "cordons bleus" of the spirit lamp even
went so far as to have elaborate cabinets—actually miniature
kitchens—equipped with wines, spices, groceries, fuel, and even
dishes and napery adorned with the symbol of the cult—a rabbit. One fin de siècle chafing dish had legs fashioned as rabbits
rampant, peering callously into the blazer and watching, with
apparent glee, the stewing of a Welsh cousin.*

*Although the chafing dish was, in those days, used for
réchauffés and Newbergs, for fondues and fudge, it was the
Welsh rabbit that ruled supreme. There was no agreement as
to how it should be made, or even how it should be spelled—
it was "rarebit" to some delicate souls—but everyone made it.
They ate it on toast, on crackers, on bacon, and even, so help*

*me, on mince pie! That last little dainty was called "slip-on."
One cannot help but suspect that it was too much even for the
trenchermen of the nineties, and that their inability to take it
played some part in the chafing dish's relegation to the attic.*

*Today the chafing dish is with us once more, and it is to be
hoped that we will be more casual in its use. Casual, for therein
lies its value. Theoretically anything that can be cooked in a
saucepan, a skillet, or a double boiler can be cooked in a chafing
dish. Actually, unless it is your only means of cooking, the
chafing dish should be reserved for definite occasions and for
definite types of cooking. Foods best suited to chafing dish
cookery are those that need little in the way of time or heat.
Fish—especially mollusks, but any seafood; innards—liver, kidneys, sweetbreads, brains; cheese, eggs, and many vegetables
are far better when cooked lightly. The chafing dish is for them.
So too, it is for the dishes that are to be served burning, in
a blaze of glory. There are some dishes which, though com-*

*monly considered adaptable to the chafing dish, I believe un-
suitable. An omelette is one, a crêpe another, a stew a third.
Proper omelettes need a shallower and differently shaped pan,
as do thin French pancakes, and both require a technique difficult to achieve with a chafing dish. As for stews and other
dishes that require long slow cooking, to use a chafing dish
would not only be expensive, it would be an affectation. Dishes
which are laboriously cooked in the kitchen and merely combined and heated in the chafing dish may be all right for a
congenital show-off, but otherwise they make little sense.
Réchauffés and salmis, on the other hand, are perfect. Not
only do leftovers seem to taste better when presented from the
chafing dish, they actually are better, for cooked meats become
rubbery-tough when subjected to too much reheating.*

*As for occasions when a chafing dish is in order—they should
be informal ones, except perhaps when the utensil is used for
some recherché dessert. The use of the chafing dish is almost a*

guarantee that the party will be fun. There will be no harried host hurrying out to the kitchen for hot appetizers, no resentful hostess missing out on preprandial gossip as she bends over a hot skillet, no delicate sauce curdled from too-high heat, no vegetable become flabby from overcooking. But there will be a delightful and relaxing atmosphere of informality and intimacy. There is no greater gesture of friendship—of true hospitality—than to allow the guests to watch the cooking.

HELEN EVANS BROWN

Pasadena, California: 1950

How to Use a Chafing Dish

THE *oldest chafing dishes, those of Ancient Troy and Greece and Rome, were braziers, charcoal-heated, as they were for many years to follow. In the seventeenth century Izaak Walton gave a recipe for fish "boiled gently over a chafing dish with coals," and a century later "chafers" were still heated with the coals from the kitchen fireplace. Just when the spirit lamp was first introduced is uncertain, though we do know that Marie Antoinettes' chafing dish was heated in this manner, "the idea having been brought from England." Alexis Soyer, the famous English chef, invented a "Magic Stove" which he predicted would be useful in "millionaires' parlours, merchants' offices, and artists' attics." It was heated with alcohol. By the time the chafing dish became the darling of the nineties, that method of heat was pretty general. Today our chafing dishes are heated with electricity, or with alcohol or Sterno.*

Most modern chafing dishes consist of a stand, almost invariably a three-legged one, the burner (electric, alcohol, or Sterno), an outer pan or water jacket, an inner pan or blazer, and a cover. The blazer is the actual cooking pan and is used for everything. When a fairly high heat and quick cooking are indicated, it is used directly over the heat as if it were a skillet or a saucepan. When longer and slower cooking is desirable the blazer is placed in the water jacket, which is in turn placed over the heat—a sort of double boiler or "bain marie." The water jacket should contain from one to two inches of water, and unless the cooking process is to be slowed considerably, it should be boiling when added. Remember that the heating power of chafing dishes varies considerably, so that cooking times given in recipes are necessarily approximate.

The main object of chafing dish cookery is the preparation of food without apparent effort; to produce that illusion everything should be assembled ahead of cooking time. All prepara-

tions that do require labor—such as parboiling, peeling, and chopping—should be done in the kitchen. If the chafing dish is your kitchen, these preliminaries may at least be attended to before the audience arrives. The tray provided for the ingredients—already measured, if you wish, and tidily arranged in bowls and pitchers—should also hold a pepper mill, a dish of salt, and sundry other seasonings, as well as a bowl of butter balls or a plate of butter, extra fuel for your chafing dish, and perhaps a little kettle of hot water. With all this at hand the cooking should proceed easily without leaving the table.

The recipes in this book are necessarily limited; chafing dish possibilities are limitless. It is hoped that the dishes that are suggested will suggest others to the cook, for the purpose of the book is to inspire rather than to instruct.

Appetizers

Salted Almonds (with variations)

Blanch a pound of almonds and dry thoroughly in a low oven. Heat ¼ cup of olive oil or butter in the chafing dish, add the almonds and cook over the direct heat, stirring often, until a beautiful amber. Drain on a tray covered with crumpled paper napkins, and sprinkle with coarse salt. The variations: Add 2 crushed cloves of garlic to the oil. Sprinkle the almonds while they are cooking with a tablespoon of curry powder, chili powder, or any dried powdered herb or spice, or fresh minced parsley, tarragon, or chives. These are to be served with cocktails, and at once. If ever you've tasted almonds really freshly roasted, you'll know why. Incidentally, any other nuts may be treated in the same manner.

"Cookery means the knowledge of all herbs and fruits and balms and spices."
JOHN RUSKIN

2

Bacon Bouchées

Oysters for these appetizers, or shrimps, or scallops, or chicken livers. Olives too. Wrap the tidbit of your choice—raw, please—in ½ slice of bacon and fasten securely with a toothpick. Sliced water chestnuts may be included in the filling, or, if pitted ripe olives are used, they may be stuffed with cheese or an anchovy. Cook, turning occasionally, in the blazer until the bacon is very crispy. Drain on paper, pour fat from the chafing dish, and return the tidbits to keep hot while serving.

"Viands of simple kinds allure the taste."
HOMER

La Bagna Cauda

This is frankly a dunk—the national sauce of Piemonte. There it is used for vegetables at table; we prefer it as an adjunct to the cocktail hour. Heat ½ cup of olive oil, ¼ pound of butter, 4 cloves of garlic and 6 anchovies that have been crushed together in a mortar. (If you don't like anchovies—poor you—try this with 6 sauté chicken livers instead.) Heat all together in the blazer and keep over hot water, allowing the guests to dip into it with crisp stalks of celery, finocchio, green pepper, or raw artichoke bottoms. Radishes, ripe olives, or fingers of toast are also good bathed with it. A small chafing dish is in order, and black ties should be covered with bibs.

"He doth learn to make strange sauces, to eat anchovies .."

BEN JONSON

4

Cheese and Walnut Balls

Mix a cup of grated Cheddar with 2 tablespoons of flour, ½ teaspoon of salt, ½ teaspoon of chili powder, ¼ teaspoon of oregano, and a beaten egg white. Roll in marble-sized balls and then in chopped walnuts and chill until cocktail time. Melt ⅛ pound of butter in the blazer, sauté balls until lightly brown on all sides, and serve on toothpicks, or in little paper bonbon cups.

"Pray, does anybody here hate cheese?
I would be glad of a bit."
JONATHAN SWIFT

Swiss Toast

This recipe from the Switzerland Cheese Association has appeared in several other books, but it's worth repeating. Mix ¼ pound of genuine Swiss cheese with a beaten egg yolk, ½ teaspoon of grated onion, a pinch of salt, and ½ teaspoon of cream. Fold in a beaten egg white (not too stiff, please) and spread the mixture on sliced rye bread, crust removed. Fry, cheese side down, in the blazer, using ⅛ pound of butter. Turn, do other side, cut bread in quarters, and serve hot with cocktails.

Nun's toast was an old-time chafing dish favorite. Bread, fried in the blazer, and sprinkled with grated cheese.

6

Roasted Chestnuts

After the preliminary work is done, these are very simple for the chafing dish, and even the preliminaries are easy if you do it this way. Boil 2 pounds of chestnuts for 10 minutes, then remove shell and skin while still hot. At cocktail time heat ¼ pound of butter in the blazer and cook the whole peeled chestnuts until lightly browned and thoroughly hot. Sprinkle with salt and a little curry powder and serve in paper bonbon cups.

"And a large chestnut, the delicious meat
Which Jove himself, were he
a mouse, would eat."

ABRAHAM COWLEY

Cocktail Balls

These can be made of almost anything in the way of meat or fish. The trick is to grind whatever it is fine, and for each well-packed cupful add a whole egg and the seasonings of your choice. Veal is good with a couple of chopped anchovies added, shrimps with water chestnuts and a touch of ginger, ham with a few ripe olives, crab with tarragon, pork with a little garlic—you get the idea? Salt, of course, and roll in marble-sized balls, then in cornstarch. Sauté in the blazer in plenty of butter and serve hot, speared on toothpicks. If sauce you must, try soy, tomato, mushroom, sour cream, or any other that suits your fancy.

"Keen appetites and quick digestion
Wait on you and yours."
JOHN DRYDEN

8

Cocktail Sandwich Bites

Make sandwiches of various savory fillings: Swiss cheese and ham; salami with Jack cheese; Camembert cheese and bacon; shrimps with curry; hard-boiled egg with ripe olives; lamb with anchovies —you know the kind. Butter both slices of bread and press the sandwiches firmly together. Then cut into bite-sized pieces and dip in a cup of milk which has had 2 eggs and a little salt mixed in. Sauté in the blazer, in butter, and serve piping hot. Man-sized paper napkins are advisable here.

" 'Man cannot live by bread alone'
  'Tis well and wisely spoken,
But make that bad, he'll die
    unknown
And give the world no token".
  ANDREW BOORDE: 1536

Scorched Codfish

Soak a thick ½-pound piece of salt cod overnight, bring to a boil, drain and pick into good-sized pieces. Dry well, then cook in a blazer with ½ cup of butter until well browned on both sides. In spite of the name, don't burn it. Sprinkle with minced chives, parsley, and thyme. Oysters, cooked in the same way until really brown, are also good as an appetizer. Serve on toast pieces with some of the brown "skin" which will form on the bottom of the chafing dish.

"There, stay thy haste
And with this savoury fish
Indulge thy taste."

JOHN GAY

Cocktail Hamburgers

These are always a favorite with cocktails, and when done in the chafing dish you can keep them hot and keep them coming. Make miniature patties of ground round steak, seasoned in your usual manner, and cook them in the blazer, in butter, turning them as you would a man-sized hamburger. Serve them on slices of French rolls that have been cut as if they were Lilliputian loaves, the slices buttered and, if you wish, spread with mustard or topped with transparent slices of tiny onions. (Some hosts prefer to form the beef into balls and serve it spiked on toothpicks.)

"Of mordant mustard add a single spoon,
Distrust the condiment
  that bites too soon."

SYDNEY SMITH

II

Lobster Balls

Put the meat of a 2-pound boiled lobster through the food chopper. Mix with the yolks of 3 hard-boiled eggs, 1 whole raw egg, a tablespoon of cornstarch, 2 tablespoons of butter, a tablespoon of milk, a little salt, and 2 teaspoons of minced tarragon and some fresh ground pepper. Roll into walnut-sized balls and then in flour. Chill, then brown in the blazer, in butter, and serve speared on toothpicks. A good dunking sauce is a cup of sour cream seasoned with 2 teaspoons of lemon juice, a little salt, and a tablespoon of chopped fennel.

*"The savoury odour blown
Grateful to appetite, more
pleased my purse
Than smell of sweetest fennel."*
JOHN MILTON

12

Lobster or Shrimps with Vermouth

Heat ¼ cup of olive oil in the blazer with a crushed clove of garlic. Add 1½ pounds of cleaned raw shrimps or the meat from a 2-pound lobster, raw or cooked, cut in sizable chunks. Cook, stirring, for 2 or 3 minutes, then add ¼ cup of French vermouth and cover. Cook for 5 minutes longer, or until the fish is done. Squeeze on the juice of half a lemon and allow the guests to snatch their own morsels from the chafing dish. Provide sourdough French rolls, sliced like bread and buttered, as a trencher. (This may also be served as an entrée.)

"Room! Make Way!
Hunger commands;
My valour must obey."
      BEAUMONT & FLETCHER

Mushrooms Bourguignonne

In the blazer, cook ½ cup of Burgundy or Pinot Noir with a crushed clove of garlic, ⅛ pound of butter, a pound of cleaned mushroom caps, a little salt and pepper, and 2 teaspoons each of minced parsley and shallots. When the mushrooms are done, which should be in about 5 minutes, serve with steak or on buttered toast, or spear on toothpicks and present with preprandial drinks.

"Taste of it first."
W. SHAKESPEARE

14

Fish Roe

Melt ⅓ cup of butter in the blazer, add a tablespoon of lemon juice, and a pound of any fish roe with the skin removed. Break the roe but don't mash, then mix in the mashed yolks of 3 hard-boiled eggs, ½ cup of dried bread crumbs, a tablespoon each of minced chives and parsley, and 2 teaspoons of minced tarragon. Season with salt and pepper and add just enough cream or sherry to make of spreading consistency. Cook long enough to heat thoroughly, then put over hot water and allow guests to spread their own—on toast or crackers. Crumbled bacon may be added if desired. Another way with roe is to wrap pieces in bacon and cook crisp in the blazer.

"You must stay the cooling,
too, or you may chance
to burn your lips."
W. SHAKESPEARE

Sardine Toasts

Cut slices of whole-wheat bread in 3 strips and butter them on one side. Cook in the hot blazer, buttered side down, until brown, turn toasts, place a whole boneless or skinless sardine on each piece, squeeze on a little lemon juice, and continue cooking until the fish are hot. Deviled ham or any meat or fish paste may be spread on the untoasted side in place of the sardines.

*"By the way, we had half a dozen sardines
while the dinner was getting ready."*
W. M. THACKERAY

16

Stuffed Shrimps

Select a pound of jumbo shrimps or prawns for this. Remove the shells and split them two-thirds of the way through the back, removing their sand veins in the process. Insert half an anchovy in each split and put the shrimps in the blazer with ⅛ pound of butter and a crushed clove of garlic and the juice of half a lemon. Cook, stirring, for 3 or 4 minutes, then sprinkle with salt and pepper, cover, and continue cooking until the shellfish are bright pink and have lost any transparent look. Serve them on pieces of well-buttered pumpernickel bread. Unless you want the guests to skip their dinner, you'd better not be too generous with these delicacies.

"The gentleman who dines the latest
Is in our street esteemed the greatest;
But surely greatest of them all
Is he who never dines at all."
A. LYMAN PHILLIPS

Entrées

Abalone in Cream

Abalone, as every gastronome knows, needs the least possible heat. That makes it right for a chafing dish, for with that low gentle fire it is a bit of a feat to overcook it. Cut a pound of abalone steaks into strips, dust lightly with seasoned flour (¼ cup flour, ½ teaspoon salt, a little fresh ground pepper), and sauté very quickly in ¼ cup of butter. Use the blazer and have it hot, and cook the mollusk not more than half a minute on each side. Add ½ cup of heavy cream and a teaspoon of lemon juice and cook another 30 seconds or long enough to heat the cream. Double-quick perfection.

"Give us the luxuries of life and we will dispense with its necessities."
OLIVER WENDELL HOLMES

18

Beef Stroganoff

Have 2 pounds of tenderloin of beef sliced thin, then cut it in strips about ½ x 2 inches. In the blazer melt ⅛ pound of butter and in it sauté a medium-sized white onion (sliced ¼ inch thick and the slices cut in halves) and ½ pound of sliced fresh mushrooms. When the vegetables are wilted, push them to one side of the pan and add the meat. Brown it quickly on both sides—this shouldn't take more than 5 or 6 minutes. Now add 2 cups of sour cream, and salt, pepper, and prepared mustard to taste. As soon as the sauce is hot, serve with rice.

"It almost makes me wish, I vow,
To have two stomachs like a cow."
THOMAS HOOD

Tournedos of Beef, with Bearnaise Sauce

You'll need a brace of chafing dishes for this one, but the one for the sauce may be small. Start the Bearnaise first. Cook ¼ cup of good tarragon vinegar with 2 tablespoons of very finely minced shallots until the vinegar is absorbed. Place over hot water and add ½ teaspoon of prepared mustard, 2 egg yolks, and ¼ pound of butter, a little at a time, stirring until the sauce thickens. Keep the flame low so that the water beneath will *not* boil. When the sauce is thick and shiny, turn off heat—or remove from the flame. In the meantime have the blazer of the larger chafing dish very hot, add 2 tablespoons of butter and 4 tenderloin steaks cut about an inch thick. Sauté quickly on one side, then on the other, and serve with the Bearnaise, which has been given a stir or two while the steaks are cooking. (If it *should* curdle, a drop or two of cream or boiling water, stirred in quickly, will bring back its good behavior.)

This sauce is superb with fish, too, or with a humble meat loaf.

"Epicurean cooks sharpen with cloyless sauce his appetite."

W. SHAKESPEARE

20

Beef Steak à la Mode

Have a pound of tenderloin steak cut an inch thick, and cook quickly in a hot blazer in 2 tablespoons of butter, on both sides. Add the juice of a lemon, ¼ cup of port, and ¼ cup of rich brown stock. Baste the meat with this sauce for a minute or two, or until done to your taste, and serve on toast. Mushrooms may be used as a garnish. The "rich brown stock" is made by cooking bouillon or consommé until it is reduced to a quarter of its original volume. This is quick and utterly perfect.

"I'll be with you in the squeezing of a lemon."

OLIVER GOLDSMITH

Grenadine of Beef with Oysters

Have 4 slices, ½ inch thick or a little less, cut from the center of the beef tenderloin. Heat 2 tablespoons of butter in the blazer, add the beef, cook quickly on both sides, remove to a hot platter. Add a cup of small oysters to the pan, cover and heat until the oysters plump. Pour them around the grenadines, sprinkle with minced parsley and salt and serve. A variation: Omit oysters, add ½ cup of sliced chicken livers and ¼ cup each of Madeira and consommé to the pan; cook 5 minutes before pouring over the grenadines.

"Sometimes with oysters we combine."
JOHN GAY

Brains with Pignolias

Parboil a set of cleaned calves brains in acidulated water for 15 minutes. Plunge into ice water, then split each brain with a sharp knife and sauté in the blazer in ½ cup of butter until lightly browned. Remove to a warm dish and sprinkle with salt. Add ½ cup of pignolias (pine nuts) to the butter and cook quickly until the butter becomes quite brown. No burning, though. Add 2 teaspoons of lemon juice, and pour, nuts and all, over the meat. This sauce, without the nuts, is the classic *beurre noir*, a favorite one for brains. Another way, adaptable for chafing dish cookery, is to add sliced parboiled brains to scrambled eggs.

"O dainty and delicious!
Food for the Gods!"
CROFFUT

Champagne Cheese

This recipe is to a Queen's taste, as it was said to have been Victoria's own. She, the story goes, made it with her own plump hands for her beloved Albert. Put the chafing dish over hot water and melt "a butter ball" (2 tablespoons of butter) in it. Add ½ pound of rich grated Cheddar and ¼ cup of champagne. Also a touch of salt. Stir while cooking slowly, and as soon as melted serve with toast and, of course, champagne.

At the turn of the century, a tidy little pyramid of butter balls was as much a requisite for the chafing dish as was a spoon. And a good idea it was, too.

24

Swiss Cheese Fondue

Recipes for cheese fondue, from Brillat-Savarin's to Fannie Farmer's, are numerous and varied, but none can excel the classic one of Switzerland: *Fondue Neuchâteloise*, it is called. Rub the blazer well with a cut clove of garlic, then pour in a cup of dry white table wine and place over hot water. When the wine is hot but not boiling, add ½ pound of grated Switzerland Swiss cheese which has been dredged with 4 teaspoons of flour. Add cheese, a little at a time, and as it melts add more. Keep stirring. Season with salt and pepper and a grating of fresh nutmeg, then stir in 3 tablespoons of Kirsch. Place in the middle of the table, still over hot water, give each guest a fork and a dish of cubed French bread and let him dunk from the common dish.

Note: The Swiss say to serve Kirsch with this meal, but white wine, perhaps Chablis or Pinot Chardonnay, not too cold, is nice, too.

Cheese Fondue

This fondue, not quite so rich, was described as one "fit only for school children" by a trencherman of the nineties. Melt 3 tablespoons of butter in the blazer, add 2 cups of grated Cheddar and a cup each of soft bread crumbs and light cream. Season with salt and a little cayenne and place over hot water, stirring, until the cheese is melted. Beat 2 eggs light, stir in and cook, whipping, just enough longer for the eggs to heat. Serve on toast which has been covered with 2 slices of crisp bacon. Another way to serve it is on English muffins spread with anchovy paste.

"Among the entremets was a simple fondue, of which the prelate helped himself copiously."

BRILLAT-SAVARIN

Breast of Chicken with Almonds

Dust the breasts of 2 young chickens lightly with seasoned flour, and sauté in the blazer, using ½ cup of butter. When beautifully colored on one side, turn and cook until tender. Remove to the side of the pan, stacking the breasts to make room. In the pan toss ½ cup of slivered almonds and brown lightly in the butter. Add ¼ cup each of sherry and cream. Heat just a minute and serve spooned over the chicken breasts.

Almonds, slivered and cooked golden in butter, are perfect on sautéed filet of sole, on asparagus, on veal cutlets, and on string beans.

Chicken Hashed in Sour Cream

Melt 3 tablespoons of butter in the blazer, and add 2 cups of finely chopped cold roast chicken and 2 cups of chopped cooked potatoes. Pour in a cup of sour cream, season with salt and pepper, and cook, stirring, over hot water until heated. Sprinkle with minced chives and serve garnished with broiled tomatoes.

"A cheerful look makes a dish a feast."
SENECA

28

Chicken Marka

Two cups of cooked chicken or turkey are needed for this unusual and delightful entrée. Cut the meat—what's left of a roast, or canned chicken if you wish—into good-sized cubes. Cook ½ cup of chopped green onions in the blazer using 2 tablespoons of butter. Add the meat—2 cups of it—along with ½ cup of sliced water chestnuts, a teaspoon of fresh ginger cut into pin-sized slivers, and a cup of sour cream. Put over hot water, season with salt, and cook gently until the meat and cream are hot. Serve with rice.

"Where love has entered as the seasoning of food, I believe it will please anyone."
PLAUTUS

Chicken with Chestnuts

Make a sauce by cooking ½ cup of minced ham and ½ cup of minced onions in ¼ cup of butter until the onion is golden, then add 3 tablespoons of flour. Cook 3 minutes, stirring well, pour in a cup each of chicken stock and cream, ¼ cup of white wine, and salt and pepper to taste. When smooth and thickened, add 1½ cups of cubed cooked chicken and a cup of boiled peeled chestnuts that have been cut in half. When all is hot serve with wild rice.

Sweetbreads, parboiled and cut in pieces, may take the place of the chicken.

Chicken with Macaroni and Olives

Melt ¼ cup of butter in the blazer, add ¼ cup of flour and cook a couple of minutes, then pour in 1 cup each of cream and rich chicken stock. Season to taste, and when smooth and thickened add a cup of diced cooked chicken, a cup of cooked elbow macaroni, and ½ cup of sliced ripe olives. A jigger of sherry or ½ cup of cheese may be added for variation. When all is smooth and thick and hot, serve it forth.

"Some nice ragout or charming fricassee."
WILLIAM KING

Deviled Drumsticks

In the days when a half-dozen pullets were sacrificed for some *suprème*, this recipe was devised to use the drumsticks. Today we can buy chicken "parts"; 6 drumsticks or second joints are needed here. Put them in a covered casserole and bake at 300° until just tender. (This will take ½ hour for very tender birds, but a knowing fork is more reliable.) No seasoning is used for plenty of that is to come. The chicken legs are allowed to become cold and are then scored deeply with a sharp knife—slashed almost to the bone, that is, in 4 or 5 places. Now each leg is rubbed with a mixture of 2 teaspoons of salt, 1 teaspoon of pepper, 1 teaspoon of dry mustard, and 2 tablespoons of flour. Melt 2 tablespoons of butter in the hot blazer, add 3 tablespoons of olive oil and the chicken legs. Cook and turn them, with heat turned high, until they are brown on all sides, then pour in a cup of chicken stock and 2 tablespoons of Escoffier Sauce Diable or Worcestershire sauce. Baste the meat a few times with the juices until all is hot, and serve with baked potatoes or noodles.

."*God sends meat and the Devil
sends cooks*."
JOHN TAYLOR: 1630

Chicken Gizzards and Livers, Chinese Style

Cut ½ cup each of raw chicken livers and cooked gizzards in pieces, along with the meat from 1 cooked pork chop, slivered. Sauté in the blazer in 2 tablespoons of bland oil or butter until the livers are lightly browned. Add a teaspoon of finely minced green ginger, ½ cup of sliced water chestnuts or raw celery, a cup of chicken stock, a tablespoon of soy sauce, and 2 tablespoons of cornstarch mixed with ¼ cup of cold water. Cook, still over the direct heat, until the sauce is transparent. Serve with rice and Chinese peas.

Chinese peas, the strings and ends removed, are cooked in another chafing dish, in a little butter, only until hot and bright green.

Chicken Livers, Flambé

Some people feel cheated if they are served something from a chafing dish that hasn't first flared to the ceiling in flames. This recipe burns cognac, not to be dramatic, but to add a lovely flavor. Dust a pound of halved chicken livers in flour, then sauté them lightly (in the blazer) in ¼ cup of butter. When they lose their red-juiced look and are delicately colored on all sides, pour on a jigger of cognac and set fire to it. When the flutters and flames subside, put the blazer over the hot water jacket, sprinkle the livers with a tablespoon of finely minced fresh tarragon (or a teaspoon of the dried, presoaked in the cream). Now pour in a cup of hot cream which has been mixed with 2 beaten egg yolks. (Mix the yolks, add the cream gradually.) Add salt to taste and as soon as the sauce thickens, serve at once on squares of fried hominy or on toast.

"'Tis better to be lowly born and range
with humble livers."
W. SHAKESPEARE

Chicken Livers with Green Olives

Cut a pound of chicken livers in halves (be sure to discard the gall) and roll them in ¼ cup of flour. Melt ⅛ pound of butter in a chafing dish blazer, add 2 tablespoons of minced shallots or green onions and the chicken livers. Stir and cook gently for 3 or 4 minutes or until the blood stops running, then add ½ cup each of white wine and chicken stock and ¼ cup of slivered green olives. Salt and pepper to taste, and if the idea pleases you, a pinch of powdered dill. Cook another couple of minutes and serve with rice and with grilled tomatoes or asparagus as the vegetable.

Dill loves olives, but if you don't like its flavor try garlic in this dish, grinding it to a nothingness in the salt.

Clam and Eggs

Melt a tablespoon of butter in the blazer, add a 7-ounce tin of minced clams and 6 eggs, beaten just enough to mix yolks and whites. Season with salt and pepper and place over the hot water jacket. Proceed as in scrambled eggs. Just before serving fold in a good-sized piece of butter. Serve on slices of eggplant that have been dipped in egg and crumbs and fried brown on both sides. This, with crisp bacon, makes a fine lunch or supper dish.

Minced clams, the kind that come canned, are almost a requisite for chafing dish cooks.

36

Hashed Clams with Sherry

Heat 2 tablespoons of butter in the blazer, add 2 cans of minced clams, 3 tablespoons of sherry, a tablespoon each of minced chives and parsley. When hot stir in a cup of cream mixed with 4 egg yolks. Cook another minute, season to taste, and serve on pastry points. Actually, almost any meat or fish can be heated in this sauce which, except for the herbs, is a Newberg. Try cubes of veal or rabbit, flaked white fish, or hard-boiled eggs.

"A genial savor of certain stews."
                    LORD BYRON

Salt Codfish in Cream

Plebian perhaps, but a great favorite with almost everyone. Make a sauce with 3 tablespoons each of butter and flour and 2 cups of cream. Add 2 cups of freshened salt codfish and cook over hot water for 10 minutes or until the fish is tender. Season with pepper, add salt if necessary, and just before dishing stir in a beaten egg. Serve with baked potatoes and fried green tomatoes.

"Of all the fish that swim or swish
In ocean's deep autocracy,
There's none possess such haughtiness
As the codfish aristocracy."

WALLACE IRWIN

38

Crab Meat with Rum Rabbit

Melt 3 tablespoons of butter in the blazer, then add a pound of Cheddar cheese and a jigger of light rum. Place over the water jacket and cook gently until melted, then fold in a pound of crab meat which has been carefully picked over. Leave over the heat just long enough for the shellfish to heat, then serve on toasted whole-wheat bread. This is, quite obviously, very rich. If too much so, ⅓ cup of milk may be added with the cheese. It will still be rich.

"There's naught, no doubt,
so much the spirit calms,
As rum and true religion."
LORD BYRON

Curried Anything

Cut a pound of any cooked meat or fish or shellfish into ½-inch cubes. Melt 3 tablespoons of butter in the blazer, add ½ cup each of chopped apple and onion, a clove of garlic that has been crushed to nothing in ½ teaspoon of salt, and a tablespoon of curry powder (more or less, suit yourself). Cook until the onion is transparent, then add a tablespoon of flour, cook another 2 minutes, pour in a cup of bouillon or stock, and add the meat or whatever you plan to sauce. Cook slowly long enough to heat and serve with rice.

If eggs are to be curried, add them, hard-boiled and quartered, after the sauce has thickened. Heat without stirring.

40

Kofta Curry

Mix together 2 pounds of ground meat (beef or lamb or veal) with
a medium onion, minced, an egg, 1½ teaspoons of curry powder,
1½ teaspoons of salt, and a teaspoon of lemon juice. Form in balls
the size of a walnut. (Here is one time when *that* culinary direction
is as accurate as one can be.) Cook another medium onion, sliced,
and a crushed clove of garlic in ⅛ pound of butter until wilted—
use the blazer for this. Remove garlic and add a tablespoon of curry
powder, 2 teaspoons of sugar, 2 tablespoons of flour, and 3 cups of
tomato juice. Season to taste with salt, more curry powder if needed
or a touch of cayenne if you can take it, and a squeeze of lemon
juice. When the sauce has thickened a bit, add the meat balls one at
a time, cover and cook for 20 minutes. Serve with rice and chutney.

*"Do you put cayenne into your cream
tarts in India, Sir?"*
            W. M. THACKERAY

Breast of Wild Duck

Split the breasts of 2 wild ducks and cook them in a very hot blazer with ⅛ pound of butter. When brown on both sides remove to a hot dish and to the chafing dish add ½ cup of Burgundy or Pinot Noir, ½ cup of very rich duck stock (made from trimmings, or if you have a duck press, made by pressing the carcass of a duck that has been roasted rare), a jigger of cognac, a little salt and cayenne, and a drizzle of lemon juice. Return duck breasts to sauce and as soon as they are well heated, serve with wild rice and plenty of Burgundy.

"An exquisite and poignant sauce, for which I'll say unto my cook, 'There's gold, go forth and be a knight'."
BEN JOHNSON

42

Duck with Madeira, Réchauffé

Pick the meat from the carcass of a cold roast duck, and cut in fairly good-sized pieces, having 2 cupfuls or a little more. Mash the cooked liver in the blazer, add the juice of ½ lemon, ½ teaspoon of salt, a little cayenne, ¼ cup of butter, ½ cup of Madeira, a tablespoon of minced parsley, and, if available, ¼ cup of duck gravy or stock. When hot add the duck pieces, and the very instant they are heated serve with buttered toast and tender green peas.

"That I may reach that happy time
The kindly Gods I pray,
For are not ducks and peas in prime
Upon the last of May."
                   W. M. THACKERAY

Browned Scrambled Eggs

A perfectly scrambled egg is a culinary achievement. It is a soft and shining mixture in which both white and yolk retain their own personalities though joining in a harmonious whole. No hint of dryness mars its beauty, yet no vestige of uncooked egg remains. Break 6 eggs into a bowl and with a fork mix them just enough to break the yolks. Season them with salt and fresh ground pepper. In the blazer, which is directly over the heat, melt ⅛ pound of butter (that's ¼ cup) and allow it to brown—but gently. It's the color of topaz you want. Now place the pan over the hot water jacket, pour in all the eggs at once, and allow them to set at the bottom. Draw the spoon across the whole width of the pan and repeat until all the egg has formed into long soft curds, creamy white, with flecks of deep gold. The instant the eggs are set serve them with plenty of thin hot toast. Snips of chives or parsley, tiny dice of Cheddar, slices of ripe olives, or morsels of crisply fried ham may be added at the last.

"They are up already and call for eggs and butter."

W. SHAKESPEARE

44

Mexican Eggs

Huevos Rancheros is the Mexican name for this particularly fine egg dish. Crush a clove of garlic and cook it, a canned green chili pepper, and a chopped onion in 2 tablespoons of olive oil until lightly browned, using the blazer. Remove garlic if you can find it, and add 2 cups of canned tomatoes. Season with salt and a speck of cuminos (optional, that), and when hot slip in 6 raw eggs. Cover and continue cooking until the eggs are set. Serve with refried beans (*frijoles refritos*).

Sometimes this sauce is cooked separately and poured around fried eggs. That's good too.

Sherried Eggs with Gruyère

Melt 2 tablespoons of butter in the blazer, add ½ cup of cream and heat. Place over hot water jacket and add ½ pound of Gruyère or Swiss cheese, grated. Stir until almost melted, then add 6 eggs, slightly mixed, and ½ teaspoon of salt. When the eggs are just beginning to set, stir from the bottom a few times. Just as the eggs are softly scrambled add a piece of butter (about 2 tablespoons or ¼ cube) and a jigger of sherry. Serve on toast that has been spread with deviled Virginia ham, or accompany with grilled ham. With asparagus this makes a delightful lunch, particularly if served with a glass of chilled vin rosé.

Swiss eggs used to be a chafing dish favorite: poach eggs in cream, sprinkle with cheese, cook another 2 minutes, serve on toast.

46

Eggs with Artichokes

Cut 3 cooked artichoke bottoms into small cubes and heat in ¼ cup of butter along with a crushed clove of garlic. Remove garlic, add 6 eggs, slightly beaten and seasoned with salt and pepper. Cook over hot water, stirring, until the proper consistency, and serve on English muffins that have been toasted and spread with deviled ham or anchovy paste.

Use canned artichoke bottoms for this, or cook your artichokes in acidulated water, then discard choke and leaves.

Eggs with Herbs

Cook ½ pound of chopped fresh mushrooms and 2 minced shallots
in 3 tablespoons of butter in the blazer until lightly browned. Add
3 egg yolks, beaten with a cup of cream, a teaspoon each of minced
chives, parsley, and tarragon, and 6 hard-boiled eggs, chopped fine.
Mix well and serve, as soon as hot, on toasted buttered cornbread.

*"To proceed then to this knowledge of
cookery, you shall understand, that the
first step thereunto is, to have knowledge
of all sorts of Herbs belonging unto the
Kitchin."*

GERVASE MARKHAM: 1683

Finnan Haddie, Delmonico

Parboil a pound of finnan haddie—first soaking it if very salty. Separate into large flakes. Put 2 cups of heavy cream in the blazer and simmer until it has thickened, then add 4 sliced hard-boiled eggs, the finnan haddie, a touch of cayenne, a teaspoon of lemon juice, and a tablespoon of butter. As soon as it is well heated, spoon on toast, sprinkle with minced parsley, and serve to an appreciative audience.

"It was a glorious supper. There were kip-pered salmon, and Finnan Haddock, and a lamb's head."

CHARLES DICKENS

Fish Filets in Herbs

Melt ¼ pound of butter in the blazer, sprinkle with 2 tablespoons of minced herbs (parsley, chives, and thyme). Lay in 1½ pounds of filet of any white fish, cut in serving pieces, pour in ½ cup of white wine, and sprinkle with salt (4 tablespoons of lemon juice may be used in place of the wine). Place cover on the dish and cook gently for about 10 minutes. Serve with potatoes hashed in cream, and asparagus.

"Chibals, or chives, have their roots part-ed, as garlick: a good pot herb, opening, but evil for the eyes."
GERVASE MARKHAM: 1684

50

Réchauffé of Fish, Anchovy Sauce

Make the sauce first, lest the fish, in the stirring, become too broken. Heat ⅛ pound of butter in the blazer with a tablespoon of anchovy paste, a pinch of thyme, and a grinding of pepper. When bubbling add 3 tablespoons of flour, cook a minute, then pour in 2 cups of thin cream and 2 teaspoons of lemon juice. Cook until smooth and thickened, then add 2 cups of any leftover fish broken in fairly large pieces. Canned salmon or tuna may be used. Cook over hot water just long enough to heat the fish, stirring as little as possible.

Adapted from an eighteenth-century recipe that began: "Take thyme, lemon, and whole pepper; boil them in a little fair water; then put in two anchovies . . ."

Green Pepper Frittata

Put 3 tablespoons of olive oil in the blazer and in it cook a crushed clove of garlic for 2 minutes. Discard garlic and add 3 green peppers, sliced, and a sliced onion. Sprinkle with salt and a little oregano, cover, and cook until the pepper has wilted. Beat 6 eggs enough to make them liquid, season them with salt and pepper, and pour over the peppers. Poke the mixture with a fork so that the eggs will run through the vegetables. When they begin to set, sprinkle the top with ¼ cup of grated Parmesan and loosen around the edges with a spatula. Turn out on a round dish and cut in wedge-shaped pieces.

This dish may be made with zucchini, tomatoes, onions, chard, or any other vegetable, proceeding in the above manner.

52

Frogs Legs

At their simple best, the frogs legs are lightly dusted with flour and sautéed in butter until golden. For 6 pairs of medium-sized legs use ⅓ cup of butter. When brown sprinkle with parsley and serve on toast with wedges of lemon. *Nymphes au vin blanc* are made by sautéing the legs as above, then adding white wine to the pan, and sometimes mushrooms and chopped shallots.

"Nymphes: the culinary name of the edible frog."

ANDRÉ SIMON: "A DICTIONARY
OF GASTRONOMY"

53

Frogs Legs, Provençal

Separate frogs legs and if very large cut each in half. For each pound melt ¼ pound of butter with a large clove of garlic, crushed. Dip the frog meat in flour and sauté in the butter until browned on both sides. Remove garlic, then add ½ cup each of tomato purée, sherry or Madeira wine, and very rich meat stock. Season with salt if necessary, pepper, and a dash of lemon juice, and serve at once with wild rice.

"If you of onyons would the
smell expell
Eat garlicke, that shall drown
the onyon's smell."

OLD RHYME

Ham and Sweetbreads

Parboil a pair of sweetbreads in acidulated water (1 quart of water and 2 tablespoons of lemon juice) for 20 minutes. Cool in ice water and cut into medium small pieces. Cut boiled or baked ham into pieces of the same size—a cup of them. Make a sauce by cooking 3 tablespoons of butter with 3 of flour for 3 minutes, then adding a cup of rich chicken stock and a cup of cream. Season to taste, add a spot of sherry if desired, whip in an egg yolk, then add the meat and cook over hot water until all is well heated. Serve this in pastry shells or on toast. Ham and oysters, another favorite, is made the same way, substituting a pint of drained and scalded oysters for the sweetbreads.

"Lay the essence of ham in the dish, and lay the sweetbreads upon it. Garnish with cocks' combs forced and stewed in the gravy."

HANNAH GLASSE: 1749

Kidneys in Champagne

Champagne, or white wine if the former seems extravagant, is just a way of dressing up a kidney stew. The trick with it, or with any kidney dish for that matter, is not to overcook it. Skin, remove cores, and slice a pound of kidneys—either lamb or veal. Slice ¼ pound of mushrooms and cook them in the blazer in ¼ cup of butter. After 3 minutes add the kidneys, salt and pepper, and ½ teaspoon of tarragon. Cook quickly for a couple of minutes, add a tablespoon of flour, cook 2 minutes longer, then add ⅔ cup of champagne. Serve as soon as heated.

> *"Kidneys a finer flavor gain*
> *By stewing them in fine Champagne."*
> **AN OLD CULINARY RHYME**

56

Kidneys Sauté Flambé

Skin and remove cores from 8 lamb kidneys and cut them in quarters. Sauté 2 tablespoons of chopped shallots or green onions in 3 tablespoons of butter for 2 minutes, add the kidneys and cook quickly on all sides. Season with salt and pepper, then pour over a jigger of cognac and, as soon as it is hot, light. When the flames burn down, add ½ cup of cream. As soon as the cream is hot, which will be almost at once, serve on squares of fried hominy with crisp bacon.

"There were eggs in napkins and crispy bits of bacon under silver covers; and there were . . . kidneys frizzling in a hot-water dish."

ANTHONY TROLLOPE

Deviled Kidneys

Mix ¼ cup of melted butter, a tablespoon of prepared mustard, 2 tablespoons of lemon juice, a tablespoon of grated onion, a tablespoon of Worcestershire sauce, and a speck of cayenne. Cook a sliced veal kidney in this for 4 or 5 minutes or until all traces of pink have disappeared. The same sauce may be used for any meat or shellfish that is to be deviled. Sprinkle with parsley before serving.

"And you, gentlemen, what do you say to some iligant divvled kidneys for yourselves?"

W. M. THACKERAY

Calves Liver, Indienne

Cut a pound of calves liver into ½-inch cubes and put in the blazer
with 3 tablespoons of butter. Cook, stirring, until lightly browned
on all sides, then add 2 tablespoons of tomato catsup, a teaspoon of
Worcestershire sauce, 2 tablespoons of sherry, a teaspoon of curry
powder, and a teaspoon of lemon juice. Sprinkle with salt and pepper and cook another minute, then serve on toast that has been
spread with chutney butter.

*Chutney butter: Cream ¼ pound of but-
ter with ¼ cup of chopped chutney—
preferably Major Grey's.*

Liver Cubes

Never is liver as good as when cooked at table. Have a pound of calf or baby beef liver sliced ¾ inch thick, then cut in cubes. Put 3 chopped shallots or green onions in a blazer with 3 tablespoons of butter, cook 3 minutes, then add the liver cubes. Sprinkle with salt and pepper, and cook *quickly* on all sides. Do not overcook—the liver is at its best when still pink and juicy within. Add 2 tablespoons of red wine and a tablespoon of minced parsley before serving.

Tarragon, finely minced, is not amiss in this dish, and, surprisingly, port may be substituted for the red wine.

Liver with Green Peppers, Chinese Style

Have a pound of calves liver sliced ½ inch thick. Cut in strips about ½ inch wide and 3 inches long and dust with cornstarch and salt and pepper. Cook quickly in the blazer in ¼ cup of oil until lightly browned, then add 1 green pepper, cut in long strips, and 4 green onions, cut the same way. Pour in ½ cup of tomato juice or beef stock, and cover. Cook 1 minute, then stir in ¼ cup of cold water, a teaspoon of soy sauce, ½ teaspoon of sugar, and a tablespoon of cornstarch, mixed together. As soon as the sauce clears and thickens, which is almost at once, serve with rice. The vegetables are not supposed to cook, just to warm through.

Try chicken livers, in place of the calves liver, with pineapple chunks and almonds added and pineapple juice in place of tomato.

Liver with Sour Cream

Have a pound of liver sliced rather thick, then cut it in serving pieces, and dust lightly with seasoned flour. Sauté a crushed clove of garlic in 2 tablespoons of butter for a minute, then discard garlic and add the liver. Cook very quickly on both sides until lightly browned and push to the side of the blazer. Pour in a cup of sour cream, a soupçon of prepared mustard, and some salt and pepper. Stir well and as soon as hot serve poured over the liver slices.

"This dish of meat is too good for any but anglers or very honest men."

IZAAK WALTON

Lobster à la Newberg

This most famous of chafing dish recipes was named for one Ben Wenberg, favored patron at Delmonico's. (The first syllable of the name was reversed, say some, because of Mr. Wenberg's extreme modesty. Others say it was because he and Delmonico's had a falling out.) Cut the meat from a 2½-pound boiled lobster, having it in good-sized chunks. Heat in the blazer in ⅛ pound of butter for 2 or 3 minutes, then add a jigger of sherry. Cook another minute before pouring in ½ cup of cream which has been mixed with 2 egg yolks. Place over hot water, season to taste with salt, a speck of cayenne, and a little fresh grated nutmeg. Stir continually, and as soon as the sauce thickens serve with triangles of toast or pastry.

This same recipe may be used for shrimps, scallops, oysters, sweetbreads, brains, or any delicate meat or fish.

Lobster Jambalaya

This is a chafing dish version of the classic Creole dish. In the blazer sauté ¼ cup each of chopped cooked ham, green pepper, and onion, in 2 tablespoons of butter. Add 2 tablespoons of flour, ½ teaspoon of salt, a dash of tabasco, 2 cups of canned tomatoes, and a pound of boiled lobster meat cut in pieces. Cook until the sauce is thickened, then set over the hot water jacket and add 3 cups of steamed rice. Serve when hot. Oysters may be added for variation.

"If we don't have no more gumbo and no more jambalaya, what hell cajun gon' eat that's any good, hein? Oh M'sieu, ça c'est awful."

GUMBO YA-YA

64

Garlic Lobster

This has all the flavor of Cantonese lobster, even though the shells are omitted for easier serving. Heat 3 tablespoons of oil in the blazer and add ½ pound of lean raw pork that has been chopped, a tablespoon of chopped green ginger (or crystallized ginger, rinsed of its sugar), and a crushed clove of garlic. Cook for 10 minutes, then add the meat of a 2½-pound lobster cut in rather large pieces across the grain, and ¼ cup of sliced water chestnuts or bamboo shoots (optional). Pour in a cup of chicken stock and a tablespoon of soy sauce, place the blazer over hot water, cover, and cook for about 10 minutes. Now mix 2 tablespoons of cornstarch with ¼ cup of cold water, and add. Stir to mix, and as soon as the sauce is clear sprinkle the lobster with 3 tablespoons of minced green onions and serve at once, with rice.

"Lack of bamboo makes one vulgar;
Lack of pork makes one thin."
SU TUNG-PO

Lobster in Butter

For all our fancy sauces, this is lobster at its best. Cut the meat, in fairly large hunks and across the grain, from a large boiled lobster. Heat ½ cup of butter in the blazer, add the lobster and a tablespoon of lemon juice, and cook until the lobster is thoroughly hot. Sprinkle with minced parsley and serve. A variation is to add ½ cup of slivered almonds before adding the lobster, and finish the dish with a cup of cream mixed with 2 egg yolks.

"Patties of lobster and almonds, mixed."
CHARLES READE

66

Mussels with White Wine

Made with "the poor man's oysters" this is an adaptation of the classic *moules marinière*. Thoroughly scrub 24 mussels and cook them in a covered kettle along with a cup of white wine, a crushed clove of garlic, 3 chopped shallots, and an herb bouquet (parsley, bay, and thyme). As soon as they are open, remove from the shells and pluck off the "beards." Strain the juice through triple cheese-cloth into the blazer and cook quickly until it is reduced to half its volume. Add 2 tablespoons of butter, a teaspoon of minced parsley, and a grinding of pepper, then the mussels. The instant they are hot, serve in deep dishes, afloat in the sauce and accompanied by hot and crusty French bread.

Some mussels have such long and brassy beards that in ancient times the filaments were woven into a cloth of "gold."

Golden Mussels

Prepare 24 to 36 mussels by scrubbing them well and cooking them in a covered pan with ½ cup of water. As soon as they steam open, which will be almost at once, remove the meat from the shells. Melt ⅓ cup of butter in the blazer, then remove from heat. Dip each mussel in the butter, then in cracker crumbs that have been seasoned with salt and pepper. Return blazer to heat, adding more butter if necessary, and sauté the mussels *quickly*, first on one side and then on the other. The instant they are golden serve with garlic sauce and lemon wedges.

Garlic sauce is made by grinding 2 cloves of garlic in a teaspoon of salt and adding it to a cup of mayonnaise.

Oyster Pan Roast

Melt ⅛ pound of butter in the blazer, add a pint of oysters, drained, and sprinkle with salt and pepper. Cover, and as soon as the oysters are plump, which is very soon indeed, serve them on toast. This is cooked oysters at their best. A pepper pan roast is made by adding ¼ cup each of minced green onions and green pepper to the butter and cooking for 2 or 3 minutes before adding the oysters.

Oyster pan roasts often have tomato catsup, Worcestershire, and vinegar added. Suit yourself.

69

Oysters in Anchovy Sauce

Cook 3 tablespoons of minced shallots or green onions in ¼ cup of butter for 3 minutes. Add ¼ cup of flour, 1 tablespoon of anchovy paste, 1 cup of bouillon, and a little freshly ground pepper. Cook until thickened, then add 1 pint of oysters and cook until the oysters are plump. Add a tablespoon of minced parsley, and serve on toast or over simply poached white fish.

"Take your oysters boiling hot, and fill rolls full, set them near the fire on a chafing dish of coals, and let them be hot through. So serve them up instead of a pudding."
"THE COMPLEAT HOUSEWIFE": 1750

Oysters Poulette

Cook a pint of oysters in the chafing dish just until they "plump." Transfer them to another dish. In the blazer heat 3 tablespoons of butter, add 3 tablespoons of flour and cook 3 minutes, then strain in the oyster juice and enough heavy cream to make 2 cups of liquid. Add ¼ teaspoon each of tarragon and chives, a teaspoon of lemon juice, and the yolks of 2 eggs which have been mixed with a little of the liquid. Add the oysters, season to taste, and serve in toast cups.

Toast Cups: Trim crusts from slices of fresh bread, butter them and press into muffin pans. Bake at 400° until crisp.

Hangtown Fry, Chafing Dish Style

This old California classic starts out by being fried oysters: Drain a pint of oysters, dry them, dip in slightly beaten egg and then in crumbs, and sauté in ½ cup of butter in the blazer. When nicely browned on both sides, pour on 6 eggs that have been lightly beaten with ¼ cup of cream and salt and pepper. Cook quickly until the eggs are set, and serve with crisp bacon. Some Californians insist that fried onions and green peppers accompany this dish. They are good, so why not?

"'Twould tempt the dying anchorite to eat."

SYDNEY SMITH

Oysters and Turkey

This is an old but wonderful combination. Melt ⅛ pound of butter in the blazer, add ½ pound of sliced fresh mushrooms and cook for 5 minutes, or until the mushrooms lose their chalky look. Add ¼ cup of flour, cook 2 or 3 minutes, then pour in 2 cups of cream. Cook, stirring, until smooth and thick, then add 2 cups of cubed cooked turkey meat and a pint of oysters that have been scalded. (Scald by putting in a colander and pouring very hot water over them. This keeps them from bleeding.) If the oysters are the tiny Olympias, leave them whole, otherwise cut them in pieces. As soon as the oysters are hot the dish is done. Serve at once on toast or fried hominy squares. A little sherry may be added if you wish.

"Enter a boiled turkey poult with a delicate white sauce."

CHARLES READE

Sweet and Pungent Pork with Almonds

This is celestial. Heat ¼ cup of oil in the blazer and add a pound of lean pork that has been cut in pieces and rolled in cornstarch. When nicely brown add a green pepper, cut into neat squares, 1 cup of canned pineapple chunks, ½ cup of pineapple juice, ½ cup of chicken stock, a teaspoon of soy sauce, ½ cup of blanched almonds (preferably Chinese almonds), and ¼ cup each of vinegar and sugar. Stir in 2 tablespoons of cornstarch mixed with ¼ cup of cold water and as soon as the sauce is thickened and clear, serve with rice.

"With a friend in the cook house you can get something to eat."

CHINESE PROVERB

Rabbit Paprika

This dish is just as good when made with chicken or with veal and the method is the same. Because it is a chafing dish recipe the meat is precooked. Sauté a sliced onion, medium-sized, in ¼ cup of butter until wilted. Add a tablespoon of good fresh paprika, 2 tablespoons of flour, and ¼ teaspoon of thyme. Cook another 3 minutes, add 2 cups of rabbit meat that has been cut from the bones in rather large pieces. Also add 2 cups of sour cream and cook over hot water until all is thick, adding salt to taste. If the sauce is too thick, pour in a little hot water. Serve with almond noodles.

Almond Noodles: Mix ½ pound of noodles, boiled, with ¼ cup of butter in which ¼ cup of chopped almonds have been browned.

Welsh Rabbit

Welsh rabbit was originally toasted cheese. Mrs. Glasse gives the recipe thus: "Toast the bread on both sides, then toast the cheese on one side, lay it on the toast, and with a hot iron brown the other side." "English rabbit," according to the same authority, was identical except that the bread was first soaked in red wine. Deshler Welch, in 1896, says, "Plates and toast and beer and glasses must be ready at your elbow. Quickly served and quickly eaten, and the grace shall be spoken after. This is the secret of a rabbit." For the recipe see *Welsh Rabbit with Oysters* on the next page.

"Heaven defend me from that Welsh fairy lest he turn me into a piece of toasted cheese."

W. SHAKESPEARE ("FALSTAFF")

Welsh Rabbit with Oysters

Make a simple Welsh rabbit by melting 2 tablespoons of butter in the chafing dish over hot water. Add a pound of rich Cheddar cheese, cut in little bits, and as it melts pour in ½ cup of beer or ale, stirring constantly. (Some persons also add 2 beaten eggs.) Season or not with a touch of dry mustard and stir faithfully. Just before the cheese is completely melted stir in a pint of small oysters that have been scalded by having boiling water poured over them. As soon as the cheese is melted, serve at once on toast. A variation is to poach the oysters, lay them on toast, and pour the rabbit over them. Serve with beer.

"Cheese stewed with ale is much easier of digestion than when toasted."

WHITEHEAD

Fried Rice with Pork

Heat ¼ cup of oil in the blazer, then add a cup of cooked pork that has been cut in shreds and 2½ cups of cold boiled rice. Cook stirring for 3 or 4 minutes or until hot, then add a diced green pepper, 6 diced water chestnuts, and 2 tablespoons of soy sauce. Cook another few minutes, then pour in 2 eggs. Stir constantly over heat for a couple of minutes, sprinkle with finely minced green onion, and serve. Shrimps, ham, crab, chicken livers, or such often take the place of the pork. The green peppers and water chestnuts are optional.

"How nice is rice!
How gentle, and how very
free from vice
Are those whose fodder is mainly rice!"
ANDRÉ SIMON: "FOOD"

Shad Roe

The simplest way with shad roe, and certainly one of the best, is to sauté it. For each pound of roe use ⅛ pound of butter and cook until nicely browned on both sides. Cover, place pan over hot water, and cook a few minutes longer to make sure that the insides are done. Serve with plenty of crisp bacon and with herb butter and wedges of lemon.

Herb Butter: Cream ½ cup of butter and mix in 1 tablespoon each of minced tarragon, chervil (or parsley), and chives.

Shad Roe with Oysters

Parboil a pair of shad roe in a quart of water, to which a tablespoon of vinegar has been added, for 5 minutes. Heat ¼ cup of butter in the blazer, add the roe, brown lightly on both sides, add another ¼ cup of butter and 2 cups of Olympia or other small oysters. Sprinkle with salt and pepper and cover. Cook until the oysters are hot and plump, and serve ½ roe to a portion, surrounded with oysters and sprinkled with parsley.

Heat parboiled roe in cream sauce, sprinkle with chopped fennel, and serve on toast.

80

Ward's Salmis

Chop 6 or 8 green onions, including the tender part of the green stems, and cook them in the blazer in 5 tablespoons of butter. Add 4 tablespoons of flour and cook long enough to remove the raw taste, then pour in a cup of red wine and a cup of stock. Add the juice of ½ lemon and the rind cut in a long spiral. Season with salt and a soupçon of cayenne. When the sauce is smooth and thickened, add slices of cold beef, mutton, venison, lamb, duck, or any meat or game, and cook just long enough to heat them, not a moment longer.

A salmis was originally a réchauffé of feathered game, the stock being made from the trimmings.

Smoked Salmon

You'll have to find a delicatessen that slices its own smoked salmon for this, for it must be ¼ inch thick. Cook a pound of it quickly, first on one side and then on the other, in a hot blazer with 3 tablespoons of butter. Serve at once with scrambled eggs for a superb breakfast dish. A variation is to put a slice on a toasted English muffin and top with a poached egg.

"Would it not be beneficial, were the average American to substitute fish for the everlasting steak and chop of a breakfast table?"

THOMAS MURREY: 1888

Buttered Salmon

Canned salmon for this, or some leftover boiled or baked. Cook 2 minced shallots in ¼ cup butter until wilted. Add 3 tablespoons of flour and cook 2 minutes to remove the raw taste. Stir in a cup of water, ¼ cup of lemon juice, and pepper and salt to taste. Now add the yolks of 3 hard-boiled eggs, mashed, and 2 cups of the salmon. Cover, put over hot water, and cook without disturbing until heated. Serve on well-buttered toasted English muffins and garnish with the chopped egg whites.

"Dried salmon must be differently man-aged ... when laid on the gridiron they should be moderately peppered."
"THE ART OF COOKERY": 1765

Sausage in Beer

This the men adore. Prick a pound of little pig sausages and cook them in the blazer until they are brown on all sides. Pour off the fat and pour on a cup of beer—flat beer will do nicely. Continue cooking until the beer has almost disappeared, then serve them at once with cheesed hominy and fried green tomatoes. Beer with this. A variation is to substitute white wine for the beer. White wine with that.

Cheesed Hominy: Heat a clove of garlic in 3 tablespoons of butter, add 2 cups of drained canned hominy, heat in the chafing dish, mix in ½ cup of grated cheese, and serve.

Scallops à la King

The à la king enthusiasts think this is the best sauce ever. This recipe may be used for chicken, turkey, sweetbreads, shrimps, or even for hard-boiled eggs if the idea pleases you. Cook ¼ pound of sliced mushrooms in 3 tablespoons of butter for 3 minutes, then add a tablespoon of flour, a cup of cream, a pound of scallops, cut in halves if large, 2 tablespoons of sherry, and salt and cayenne to taste. Cook until the scallops are well heated but don't allow them to shrivel, then beat 2 egg yolks with a little of the sauce and add to the mixture in the chafing dish along with 2 canned pimientos cut in strips. Heat and serve with triangles of pastry.

Pilgrims visiting the shrine of St. James bear scallop shells in token of their faith. In France the shellfish is known as "coquilles Saint-Jacques."

Panned Scallops

Overcooking is the ruination of a scallop. The delicate little mollusk resists anything but the gentlest of handling by shriveling into a rubbery travesty of its tender self. Use a pound of fresh or frozen scallops—the latter defrosted—and towel them until quite dry. Put the blazer of the chafing dish directly over the heat, add ¼ cup of butter, and when it is melted, but before it bubbles, drop in the scallops. Sprinkle with a bit of salt—½ teaspoon should do it—and a grinding of pepper. Turn the scallops gently with your wooden spoon, and when they lose their transparent look, which will be soon, squeeze on the juice of ½ a small lemon or add a jigger of dry white wine. Sprinkle generously with finely minced parsley, give the dish another turn or two over the heat, and serve them forth in their simplicity.

"And luscious scallops to allure the taste
Of rigid zealots to delicious feasts."
JOHN GAY

Seafood Newberg with Mushrooms

Remove the meat from a 2-pound boiled lobster and cut it in rather good-sized pieces across the grain. Shell a pound of green shrimps and remove the black veins. Clean a pound of mushrooms and a pound of scallops, cutting either of them in halves if they are very large. In the blazer melt ⅛ pound of butter, add shrimps and mushrooms, and cook 5 minutes. Then add lobster and scallops, allowing them to heat for a minute before pouring on a jigger of brandy and lighting it. When the flames die down, put the blazer over the hot water jacket and add a cup of hot and heavy cream which has been beaten into 4 egg yolks. Season with salt, a suspicion of cayenne, and a grating or two of nutmeg, then stir constantly until the sauce thickens. Serve at once with toast.

"In cooking fowl, or flesh, or fish,
  Or an nice or dainty dish,
With care peruse this useful book,
  'Twill make you soon a perfect cook."
"THE COMPLETE ENGLISH COOK": 1762

Celestial Shrimps with Walnuts

This is a Chinese recipe, so it calls for rice as an accompaniment. Cook 2 pounds of green shrimps, remove shells and sand veins. Put ½ pound of walnut halves in a 450° oven for 6 minutes, then rub off the brown skins—a stiff brush will help in this operation. Cut 6 green onions into thin diagonal slices and cook them in the blazer for a minute along with 2 tablespoons of butter. Pour on 2 cups of hot chicken stock, bring to a boil, add 3 tablespoons of cornstarch which has been mixed with 3 tablespoons of soy sauce, and cook until thickened and clear. Add the shrimps and the walnuts, heat for the merest minute, and serve. Blanched almonds may be used instead of the walnuts, lobster meat instead of the shrimp.

"In ordinary life you must be economical; when you invite guests you must be lavish."

CHINESE PROVERB

88

Shrimps Creole

Cook 3 tablespoons each of chopped onion, green pepper, and red pepper, and ½ cup of sliced mushrooms, in ½ cup of butter for 5 minutes. Stir in ¼ cup of flour, cook until lightly colored, then add a cup of tomato purée, ½ cup of sherry, and ½ cup of rich brown stock. Toss in a pound of cooked cleaned shrimps and cook until the sauce is thickened and the shellfish hot. Season with salt and a dash of tabasco and serve with rice.

"Chaqu'n connain ça qua pé bouilli dans so chaudière."
OLD CREOLE SAYING

Shrimp Foo Yung

Eggs foo yung is perfect for the chafing dish provided it is made in one large cake rather than in the individual sizes. Heat a tablespoon of oil in the blazer, add the meat from a pork chop (cut in shreds) and a cup of raw shredded shrimp (or any meat or fish). Cook 4 or 5 minutes, add ½ cup of bean sprouts, 3 green onions, and 2 stalks of celery, shredded, and, if you have them, ¼ cup of shredded water chestnuts. Add another tablespoon of oil and stir over the direct heat for 2 minutes or so, then mix in a tablespoon of soy sauce. Beat 6 eggs lightly and pour over vegetables, allowing it to run through to the bottom, and lifting the edges as for an omelette. When set, fold and turn out on a dish and serve with sauce.

Sauce: 1 cup of chicken stock, 4 teaspoons of cornstarch, 1 tablespoon of soy sauce, cooked until clear.

Shrimps Victoria

Shell a pound of raw shrimps and remove the black veins. Sauté them in the blazer, along with ¼ cup of minced onion, in ¼ cup of butter until the shrimps are pink. Add ½ pound of fresh mushrooms that have been cleaned and cut in quarters, and cook for 5 minutes longer, still over the direct heat. Sprinkle with a tablespoon of flour, a teaspoon of salt, and some fresh ground pepper, and cook 2 minutes, then fold in a cup and a half of sour cream. As soon as the sauce is hot serve it forth with rice or with toast.

"Off, off with my head—split
my shell into three—
I'm a shrimp! I'm a shrimp—
to be eaten with tea."
ROBERT BROUGH

Sweet and Sour Shrimps with Ginger

Even if you are dead set against sweetness or fruitiness with fish, this combination may convert you. Have 2 pounds of shrimps shelled and cleaned. Leave them whole unless they are jumbos, in which case split them. Have also 2 cups of canned pineapple chunks, 2 tablespoons of slivered green or crystallized ginger, and ½ a green pepper, cut in long strips. Cook the shrimps for 5 minutes in 3 tablespoons of butter, add the other ingredients and ½ cup each of vinegar and sugar, a cup of pineapple juice, and a tablespoon of soy sauce. Cook 2 minutes longer, then add 2½ tablespoons of cornstarch mixed in ½ cup of water. Add salt if necessary. Serve with rice as soon as the sauce is thick.

"Yes, by Saint Anne, and ginger shall be hot i' the mouth, too."

W. SHAKESPEARE

Squabs, Tarragon

Have 2 squabs split for broiling and remove backbone with poultry
shears. Heat ⅛ pound of butter (¼ cup) in the blazer, sprinkle
with a tablespoon of finely minced tarragon and lay in the squabs,
skin side down. Cook until nicely browned, turn, and cook other
side, sprinkle with salt and pour in ½ cup of dry white wine.
Cover and cook another few minutes, or until the squabs are
perfectly tender. Serve on toast and accompany with a slightly
chilled white wine. Small game birds such as quail or Cornish Rock
Hens may be done in the same manner.

*"Found the fowl duly brown, both back
and breast."*
ROBERT BROWNING

Sukiyaki

Have these ingredients ready in separate bowls: 1 pound of round steak cut in paper thin slices; 6 green onions, shredded; ½ cup of sliced mushrooms; ½ cup of shredded bamboo shoots; a soy bean cake; ½ cup of "tangle" (Japanese seaweed, available in tins) or spinach; ½ cup of Chinese cabbage, cut in shreds, and 1 cup of cooked long rice, or Shirataki, sometimes called Yam Noodles. This is available in cans. Heat 3 tablespoons of oil in the blazer and cook the meat in it. Add ½ cup of stock and 2 to 4 tablespoons of soy sauce, with a teaspoon of sugar. Now add the vegetables, keeping them in more or less separate piles, and cook until they are well heated but still have crispness. Serve with rice. Each guest helps himself directly from the chafing dish, using chopsticks, of course. This list of ingredients is intended as a guide, omit or add to your belly's content.

Sukiyaki—pronounced skyaki—is nice served with sake, the latter in thimble-sized cups.

94

Sweetbreads or Brains with Walnuts

Heat a cup and a half of heavy cream in the blazer. Add 2 cups of sweetbreads or brains that have been precooked, cooled, and cut in cubes. Also add ½ cup of sliced walnuts. Beat the yolks of 4 eggs with ¼ cup of sherry, season with ½ teaspoon of salt and a very little cayenne, and add, stirring until the sauce thickens. Serve at once with pastry points.

"The sauce is costly for it far exceeds the cates."

GREENE

Sweetbreads in Butter with Filberts

Parboil 2 pairs of sweetbreads, clean, and then split each in half. Cook in the blazer in ⅓ cup of butter until lightly browned. Season and pile them at one side of the pan. Slice a cup of blanched filberts and brown them in the blazer, adding a little more butter if necessary. Dish sweetbreads or brains on thin slices of ham or toast, put filberts on top, and pour over a sauce made by adding ½ cup of Madeira and ¼ cup of triple-strength consommé to the butter in the pan.

"My soul tasted that heavenly food, which gives new appetite."

DANTE

Tongue Ragoût

Cook a cup of sliced mushrooms in 2 tablespoons of butter, along with a tablespoon of minced shallots, for 5 minutes. Add 2 tablespoons of flour, ¾ cup of water in which a fresh tongue has been boiled, ¼ cup of sherry, ¼ teaspoon of marjoram, and salt and cayenne to taste. Add cold sliced tongue to this, and as soon as well heated serve sprinkled with minced parsley. Cold cooked meats should never be allowed to boil in a sauce, for they will toughen.

"Tongue; well, that's a very good thing when it ain't a woman's."
CHARLES DICKENS

Tripe Creole

Sauté in the blazer a large minced onion, a clove of garlic, and a large green pepper, also minced, using ⅓ cup of butter. When the onion is beginning to color add a pound of preboiled tripe, cut into strips and floured. Brown lightly, then pour in ½ cup each of tomato purée and white wine. Season with salt, pepper, a dash of tabasco, a few drops of lemon juice, and ¼ teaspoon of thyme. Cook for about 15 minutes over the hot water jacket. Serve with the inevitable rice.

Tripe is often available "prepared" or preboiled. If not, cook it until tender in acidulated water.

Tripe and Oysters

Man's food—this. Cut a pound of prepared tripe (see note on previous page) into cubes and scald a pint of drained oysters by pouring boiling water over them. Heat ¼ cup of butter in the blazer and in it cook 3 tablespoons of chopped onion until wilted. Add ¼ cup of flour, cook, stirring, for 2 or 3 minutes, add ½ teaspoon of thyme and 2 cups of thin cream, as well as the juice drained from the oysters. Heat until smooth, season with salt and pepper, then add the tripe. Cook until it is well heated, then add the oysters and serve as soon as they are plump.

"Blest be those feasts with simple plenty crowned."

OLIVER GOLDSMITH

Turkey and Chestnuts in Sour Cream

This is a fine way to use the pickings of a holiday bird. For 2 cups of meat, cut in not-too-small pieces, boil and shell ½ pound of chestnuts and cut in half. In the blazer cook ¼ cup of chopped onions in ¼ cup of butter, until wilted. Add a teaspoon of minced parsley, ¼ teaspoon of rosemary, and 3 tablespoons of flour. Cook a few minutes, then pour in ¼ cup of red wine and ½ cup of turkey stock. Stir a minute before putting in the meat and chestnuts and a cup of sour cream. Mix, season to taste with salt, and serve as soon as hot.

This is also a wonderful way to reheat leftover venison or other game.

100

Blanquette of Veal and Ham

Technically a *blanquette* is a white stew. This, made from leftover meats, is the chafing dish way. Make a cream sauce by melting 3 tablespoons of butter in the blazer, then adding 3 tablespoons of flour and cooking 2 or 3 minutes. Stir in 1½ cups of thin cream and cook until thickened. Fold in 1 cup each of diced cooked veal and ham, and ¼ cup of white wine that has been added to 2 beaten egg yolks. Cook gently for a minute or so longer, sprinkle with minced parsley, and serve on toasted English muffins. Minced herbs of your choice may also be added.

This is really a basic recipe. Tongue, or minced clams, or sweetbreads, or chicken, or a combination of any of them may be used.

Veal Pan Pie

Mix 1¼ cups of minced cooked veal with 2 chopped anchovies, a tablespoon of grated onion, and a batter made with 2 eggs, a cup of flour, a teaspoon each of salt and baking powder, ¼ teaspoon of marjoram, and ½ cup of milk. Melt ⅛ pound of butter in a hot blazer, pour in the batter all at once, and cover. Cook for 10 minutes or until the bottom is nicely browned, turn (you'll need a couple of spatulas for this) and cook on the other side, slipping a little more butter under the pie if necessary. Serve in wedge-shaped pieces.

"A cook is quite as useful as a poet,
And quite as wise, and these anchovies
show it."

EUPHRON

Réchauffé of Venison

Have thick slices of leftover roast venison trimmed, and either heat them very quickly in a little butter in the blazer and serve with the sauce, or preferably, make the sauce in the blazer, then add the venison. Serve as soon as it is hot. Do *not* boil the sauce after the meat is added. Francatelli's Venison Sauce: 2 tablespoons of port wine, a small stick of cinnamon, bruised, the thin rind of a lemon, ½ pound (1 cup) of red currant jelly. Boil for 5 minutes.

"In venison gravy, currant jelly,
 Mix with old port, see Francatelli."
    OLD COOKERY RHYME

Tournedos of Venison

Have 4 boneless venison filets cut from the loin. They should be 1 inch thick. Dip them in melted butter, then cook in the blazer which has been made very hot. Serve with Sauce Robert: Cook ½ cup of minced onion in your second (?) chafing dish, using the blazer and 3 tablespoons of butter. Add ¾ cup of very rich brown stock, 2 teaspoons of prepared mustard, a tablespoon of red wine vinegar, and a teaspoon of minced parsley. Cook quickly to reduce, and strain over the venison. If you have but one chafing dish, cook the venison in the kitchen skillet, or in an electric one at the table.

*"One cut from venison to the heart can speak
Stronger than ten quotations from the Greek."*
PETER PINDAR

Venison Hash

This recipe will do quite as well for hash of any kind of meat or fowl or game. Cook, in the blazer, ½ cup of minced onions, preferably green ones, in ¼ cup of butter. Add 2 cups of coarsely chopped cooked venison—or what have you—a tablespoon of flour, ½ cup of leftover gravy or stock, ½ cup of red wine, salt and pepper to taste, and a tablespoon of minced parsley. Simmer until well heated and serve on toast.

"What's there? Things for the cook, sir;
but I know not what."

W. SHAKESPEARE

Vegetables

Brandied Carrots

Scrape a pound of good-sized carrots and cut them in very thin, very diagonal slices. Put them in the blazer with 3 tablespoons of butter, 3 tablespoons of water, a little salt, and 2 tablespoons of brandy. Cover and cook until the liquid is absorbed and the carrots just tender but still crisp. Add another tablespoon of butter and some minced parsley and serve with liver and bacon.

"*Crowd not your table;*
Let your number be
Not more than seven,
Never less than three."
WILLIAM KING

Chinese Vegetable Cookery

The Chinese are unsurpassed at the art of vegetable cookery. They do it very quickly, watching every second. That is easy with a chafing dish. This recipe is for asparagus, broccoli, string beans, or carrots. Peel off any tough part or skin and cut into thin diagonal slices. Put 3 cups of vegetable slices in the blazer with 2 tablespoons of oil (add a crushed clove of garlic, if desired), stir 2 minutes, add 2 tablespoons of water and cover. Cook until the color of the vegetables has intensified and they are tender-crisp. Add ½ cup of stock, ¼ cup of water, a tablespoon of soy sauce, and a tablespoon of cornstarch. Serve as soon as the sauce becomes translucent.

Sliced water chestnuts, bamboo shoots, or green onions may be added to any of the vegetables.

Sweet Corn with Green Peppers

A hot vegetable dish is often the solution for an otherwise cold supper of sliced meats and salad. This would be good with baked ham, tomatoes stuffed with cottage cheese, and beer. Cut 2 cups of corn from the uncooked cobs, being careful not to include any of the hull. In the blazer cook ¼ cup of minced green pepper and 2 tablespoons of minced onion in ¼ cup of butter until wilted. Add 2 tablespoons of flour, cook 2 minutes, then add a cup of heavy cream, salt, and chili powder to taste, and the corn. Set over hot water and cook until thickened. A good way to prepare the corn is to score the rows lengthwise, through the middle of the kernels, then scrape with the back of a knife. A variation with a Mexican touch is to substitute ½ cup minced canned green chiles for the green pepper and omit the chili powder.

"Corne, which is the staffe of life."
EDWARD WINSLOW: 1595-1655

108

Lima Beans with Mushrooms

Use either frozen or canned lima beans for this, or boil fresh ones ahead of time. For each 3 cups heat 4 tablespoons of butter in the blazer and add a tablespoon of minced green onions and a cup of sliced mushrooms. After 5 minutes add the beans, salt and pepper to taste, and ½ cup of heavy cream. Cook for another 3 minutes and serve, preferably with ham. Or use sour instead of sweet cream.

*"They tempt me, your beans there: spare
a plate."*

ROBERT BROWNING

Mushrooms in Sour Cream

This unctuous sauce is sheer perfection when combined with the delicacy of the fungi. Clean a pound of fresh mushrooms, and if large cut in quarters or halves, or slice. Cook 2 tablespoons of chopped shallots or green onions in ¼ cup of butter in the chafing dish blazer. When the shallots look semi-transparent, add the mushrooms and cook for 5 minutes, stirring them now and then. Sprinkle in a tablespoon of flour, cook another 2 minutes, then add a cup of sour cream and salt and pepper to taste. (Sherry may be included, if you wish.) As soon as the sauce is hot and smooth, serve with almost anything—as a vegetable, as a sauce, as the *pièce de résistance*. 1 ½ cups of cooked diced ham or chicken livers added to it makes it a nice entrée.

"Muse, sing the man that did to Paris go,
That he might taste their soups and
mushrooms know."

WILLIAM KING

Mushrooms Provençal

Clean a pound of mushrooms and remove the stems. Cook the caps in the blazer in 3 tablespoons of olive oil for 5 minutes, then remove and set aside. In the blazer put the stems, chopped, a large clove of garlic, minced very fine, 3 shallots, also minced, and another tablespoon of olive oil. Cook 3 minutes, add a tablespoon of flour, 2 teaspoons of minced parsley, ½ teaspoon of minced thyme, ¾ cup of white wine, a tablespoon of tomato paste, and salt and pepper to taste. Cook slowly for 10 minutes or so, then add the mushrooms and reheat. Serve with cocktails, on toothpicks, or as a sauce with steak.

"Mushrooms, thought I, are better than these tasteless truffles, and so ordered a dish to try. You know what a Provençal sauce is?"

W. M. THACKERAY

III

Stewed Mushrooms

Clean a pound of mushrooms and, if large, cut into halves or quarters, stems and all. Melt ¼ cup of butter in the blazer, add the mushrooms, and cook for 2 minutes, stirring them gently. Sprinkle with salt and pepper, then pour in ½ cup of heavy cream. Cover and continue to cook for 5 minutes longer. Serve as a vegetable, or serve for breakfast with crisply toasted English muffins, broiled liver and bacon, and grilled tomatoes. Serve cream cheese and black currant jam too, and start the meal with strawberries and champagne. It's a party!

"And we must glorify a mushroom!"
BEN JONSON

Stuffed Mushrooms

These are truly wonderful either as the *pièce de résistance*, as one of the dishes at a Chinese meal, or as an appetizer. Grind a pound of raw pork and mix it with ½ cup of chopped water chestnuts, 2 tablespoons of cornstarch, an egg, ¼ cup of chopped onion, and a teaspoon of salt. Work this well together, then stuff large mushroom caps with the mixture. When ready to cook put ½ cup of chicken stock, a tablespoon of soy sauce, and 2 tablespoons of oil in the blazer. Add the mushrooms, stuffed side up, cover, and cook for 30 minutes or so, adding more stock if necessary.

"Mushrooms are the gift of nature, but a good cook is the gift of God."
                    COOKE: "EDIBLE AND
                    POISONOUS MUSHROOMS"

Mushrooms with Ripe Olives

Slice a pound of fresh mushrooms and cook for 4 minutes in ¼ cup of olive oil with a crushed clove of garlic, using the blazer. Remove garlic and add a cup of sliced ripe olives, ½ cup of tomato purée, 2 tablespoons of sherry, and a tablespoon of beef extract. As soon as all is hot sprinkle with the juice of half a lemon and some chopped parsley. Serve with steak or chops, or on toast for lunch. It may be topped with a poached egg. Dill or tarragon added to this dish is a pleasant variation.

"When the moon is at the full
Mushrooms you may freely pull;
But when the moon is on the wane
Wait ere you think to pluck again."
ENGLISH FOLK RHYME

114

Hash Browned Potatoes with Sesame

Melt 4 tablespoons of butter in the blazer and add a tablespoon
of minced shallots. When wilted add ¼ cup of sesame seeds, and
cook them until delicately colored, then add 4 large baked potatoes
that have been cut into minute—and neat—cubes. Sprinkle with a
teaspoon of salt, a grinding or two of fresh white pepper, and ¼
cup of heavy cream. Cook, stirring now and then, until the
potatoes are a golden brown. Superb!

*Sesamum Oiler, which is a Chinese oil
made from toasted sesame seeds, is even
better than butter in this dish.*

Lyonnaise Potatoes

Cook 2 tablespoons of minced green onions in ¼ cup of butter in the blazer, until wilted. Add 2 cups of diced cooked potatoes, and salt and pepper to taste. Stir gently to mix, but do not mash, and add a tablespoon of white wine vinegar. When well heated add a tablespoon of minced parsley, mix once more, and serve. These are good for breakfast, lunch, or dinner.

*"Leeks to the Welsh, to Dutchmen
butter's dear,
Of Irish swains potato is the cheer."*
JOHN GAY

Potatoes with Celery in Cream

Chop a cup of the tender green leaves and outside stalks of celery, and heat in 3 tablespoons of butter in the blazer for 3 minutes. Add 3 cups of chopped cold baked potatoes, salt and pepper, and a cup of rich cream. Cook, stirring, until all is hot. Serve with grilled mutton chops and Cumberland Sauce: Heat a cup of port wine with ½ cup of currant jelly. Cut the very outside—the zest—of half an orange in shreds, and add, along with ¼ cup of orange juice, a tablespoon of vinegar, and a little salt and cayenne.

*"As without flattery there were
no society,
So without sauces there were
no gastronomy."*
G. H. ELLWANGER

Chinese Spinach

When barbecued spareribs, cooked at the charcoal grill, are the *pièce de résistance*, this vegetable dish may be made in the patio in the time it takes to toss off a final martini. The spinach, a couple of pounds of it, will have to have been washed and blanched—the latter to reduce its bulk. (Simply plunge in boiling water for a few seconds, then drain.) Now to the chafing dish: Crush a large clove of garlic and heat in the blazer with 2 tablespoons of bland oil. Remove garlic, add well-drained spinach, and cook, turning, until the spinach is bright green and wilted. Pour in—believe it or not—a jigger of Bourbon whisky and 2 tablespoons of soy sauce. Heat another few seconds and serve.

The Chinese would add a piece of fermented bean cake to this; a piece of bleu cheese gives much the same effect.

118

Yams Flambé

This is party fare—particularly good with a holiday turkey. Scrub 2 large red yams and boil them in their skins until barely tender. Peel and cut in ½-inch slices, then cook them in the blazer in ¼ cup of butter until browned on both sides. Sprinkle with salt and with ¼ cup of brown sugar, pour on 2 jiggers of Jamaica rum, and, as soon as the rum is hot, light it. Serve when the flames die down.

"Banish that fear; my flame
can never waste,
For love sincere refines
upon the taste."
COLLEY CIBBER

Desserts

Almond Fried Cream

Although this entire dish may be prepared in the chafing dish, it is simpler to do the preliminaries in the kitchen. Scald 2 cups of heavy cream with a tablespoon of rum, a pinch of salt, 4 tablespoons of brown sugar, and ¼ cup of ground almonds. Cook over hot water with ¼ cup of cornstarch moistened in ¼ cup of milk and 4 egg yolks. When thick and smooth, pour in a shallow pan and chill, then cut in squares, dip in egg and crumbs, and again chill. Fry in deep fat at 375° until brown, then transfer to the chafing dish. Just before serving pour on 2 jiggers of rum or cognac and set afire. Pass the powdered sugar. This dish takes skill and practice. Some cooks add an envelope of plain gelatine, melted, to the cream mixture. This makes for easier handling.

"The daintiest last to make the end more sweet."

W. SHAKESPEARE

120

Spiced Grilled Almonds

Blanch a pound of almonds and dry in a warm oven. In the blazer
cook a cup of sugar, ¼ teaspoon each of cinnamon and cloves, and
¼ cup of water until it "threads." Add the almonds, and cook,
stirring, until they change color very slightly. Put out the flame
and stir until they "sugar," then put on a plate to cool. Serve with
after-dinner coffee.

*"Make your transparent sweetmeats
truly nice
With Indian sugar and Arabian spice."*
WILLIAM KING

Apple Fritters

Or *Beignets de Pommes*, if you insist. Peel and core 4 pippin apples and slice them about ⅜ of an inch thick. Cover them with Jamaica rum and allow to stand 3 or 4 hours. Drain (save that rum!) and dip in flour and then in slightly beaten egg. Sauté the apple slices in an inch of melted butter in the blazer and serve, piping hot, with powdered sugar or with rum sauce. If you wish, the slices may be dipped in a thin fritter batter (2 well-beaten eggs, ⅔ cup of milk or water, 1 tablespoon of rum or brandy, 1 tablespoon of melted butter, ½ teaspoon of salt, and 1 cup of flour) instead of in the flour. In this case they should be *dried* before dipping.

"Tarrant ventured to intimate the apple fritters were very fine."

HENRY JAMES

123 correction:

122

Brandied Apples

Apples and brandy don't have to be set afire to be spectacular. Peel, core, and slice 3 tart apples—they should be about ⅓ of an inch thick. Soak them for about 4 hours in brandy (or rum) to cover. Drain and dry them, then dust lightly with flour. Melt ¼ cup of butter in the blazer and sauté the apples, first on one side, then on the other, until brown, adding more butter if necessary. When a lovely amber, serve them piping hot. Pass a shaker of powdered sugar and a bowl of sour cold cream. If so desired, a hard sauce flavored with the brandy marinade may be served instead of the sugar and cream, and there is no reason why they *shouldn't* be served flambé.

"How we apples swim."
JONATHAN SWIFT

Apricot Soufflé with Strawberries

Beat the yolks of 5 eggs until light, then add ⅓ cup of very fine granulated sugar and a tiny pinch of salt. Fold in ½ cup of apricot preserves and 2 tablespoons of Jamaica rum. Beat the 5 egg whites stiff and fold into the other mixture. Put a piece of butter on the end of a fork and rub it on the sides and bottom of a hot blazer. Add the mixture, cover, and place over the hot water jacket. Cook gently for 25 minutes or until set. Remove cover and hot water jacket. Sprinkle top with ¼ cup of finely chopped toasted almonds, cook another 2 minutes, pour on a jigger of hot rum, and serve, flaming. Pass cold strawberries and powdered sugar.

"Spreads and sweets in puff'd prosperity."
ALEXANDER POPE

Fried Bananas with Gin

Peel 4 bananas and split lengthwise, and then in half crosswise. Dust with flour and sauté in ⅛ pound of butter in the hot blazer. When brown on one side, turn and brown on the other. Now, surprisingly enough, pour on 2 jiggers of *gin* and set afire. As soon as the flames die down, serve at once, with a muffineer, or shaker, filled with powdered sugar. If you prefer, rum or brandy may be burned instead of the gin. Very cold whipped or sour cream is good with this dessert.

"There is something in this more than natural."

W. SHAKESPEARE

Cherries Jubilee

Reduce a cup of the juice from canned pitted cherries to one-third its original volume. Return the drained cherries to the hot juice, add ½ cup of hot brandy, and set a-burning. Pour, flaming merrily, over vanilla ice cream. A tiny drop of almond extract added to the syrup is not amiss. Any canned fruit, or poached fresh fruit, may be treated in this fiery manner. Some cooks thicken the syrup with a little arrowroot before the flaming.

"Bless my soul! Our words used to come out like brandied cherries; but now a sentence is like strawberry jam."

CHARLES READE

Burnt Chestnuts

Boil a pound of chestnuts for about 10 minutes, then remove shells and inner skins while still warm. Put in a blazer with a cup of brown sugar, ½ cup of water, and a tablespoon of butter. Cook, stirring gently, until glazed and brown, then pour on ½ cup of rum or brandy and set afire. Serve, flaming, on vanilla ice cream, or with *crème brûlée*.

"Then farewell heat and welcome frost."
                    W. SHAKESPEARE

Cheese Blintzes

Make thin crêpes as in the following recipe, reserving a little of the batter. For the filling mix 2 cups of dry cottage cheese (drained, that is) with a beaten egg, 2 teaspoons of sugar, a speck of salt, and either a teaspoon of grated orange rind or ¼ teaspoon of cinnamon. Put a spoonful on each crêpe, fold like an envelope, and seal edges with reserved batter. Chill until serving time, then sauté in the blazer in ¼ cup of butter. Serve with sour cream and preserved cherries.

Crêpes, filled with rum-flavored apricot jam, and served with sour cream, are superb.

Crêpes with Liqueur Sauce

I do not believe that French pancakes can be properly made in the chafing dish, even if it is equipped with a "suzette" pan. Make the crêpes beforehand in the kitchen, using a small buttered frying pan and putting a tablespoon of batter in it at a time, then turning and tilting so that the batter will spread thinly over the bottom. The batter is made by beating 3 eggs, adding ¾ cup of milk, ¾ cup of flour, 2 tablespoons of melted butter, 1 tablespoon of cognac, ½ teaspoon of salt, and, when used for dessert, a teaspoon of sugar. For a sauce use ½ cup of your favorite liqueur, and heat in the blazer with ¼ cup of butter and ¼ cup of sugar. When the sauce is syrupy, add the crêpes, heat, and serve at once.

" *'Tis the dessert that graces all the feast,*
For an ill end disparages the rest".
WILLIAM KING

Crêpes Suzette

I dare not omit this recipe, for many believe it is the *raison d'être* of the chafing dish. Make 18 very thin French pancakes and keep warm (on a bowl-covered plate, over hottish water) until dessert time. Make a butter by creaming ½ pound of sweet butter with the grated rind of a lemon and an orange, and 3 tablespoons of powdered sugar. Chill until needed. Then put in the blazer of the chafing dish, and when bubbling gold add the juice of an orange. When the juice is well reduced, add 2 jiggers each of Cointreau and Grand Mariner. Dip the crêpes in this mixture, one at a time, and fold in quarters, putting each one as it is done at the side of the dish. When all are folded sprinkle with a little sugar and pour on two jiggers of brandy or rum, then set alight. Serve about 3 to a portion with a little of the flaming sauce poured on.

Some prefer Benedictine, Curaçao, Kirsch, or Maraschino in their liqueur mixture.

130

Flaming Figs

If ripe figs are available, split 8 of them and sauté in the blazer in plenty of butter. Pour on a jigger or 2 of brandy and set afire. Serve hot with a shaker of powdered sugar and, if you wish, with ice cream. If dried figs are the only kind procurable, soak ½ pound of them in brandy overnight, then stuff with blanched almonds, press flat, and sauté in the blazer in ¼ cup of butter until lightly colored. Add the brandy in which they soaked, and light. When the flames burn down add ½ cup of very heavy cream and a speck of salt, then serve at once with a plain cookie or a ladyfinger.

"In the name of the Prophet, figs!"
HORACE SMITH

French Toast or Pain Perdu

They were making this back in the fifteenth century. *Payn-Pur-Dew*, the recipe was called, and it began, "Take fayre yolkys of eyrouns," which meant take good yolks of eggs. Centuries later Mrs. Glasse called it *Pain perdu, or cream toasts*. Today we call it *French toast*, not quite understanding why it was ever lost. It's never better than when cooked, in butter, under hungry noses. Trim crusts from stale bread, dip in a mixture of 1 cup of rich milk, 2 eggs, a teaspoon of sugar, and ½ teaspoon of salt, and fry in the blazer in plenty of butter.

Serve this with preserves, for dessert, or with syrup, for breakfast.

132

Rum Omelette

This "soufflé" omelette is the only type of omelette that can be properly made in a chafing dish. Beat the yolks of 4 eggs until very light, then beat in ¼ teaspoon of salt, 4 tablespoons of sugar, and 2 tablespoons of Jamaica rum. Now beat the whites stiff and fold them into the yolks. Heat the blazer well and rub the entire inside with a cube of butter, then pour in the egg mixture. Cook as quickly as possible, running a spatula around the sides of the pan. When set, fold in half, sprinkle with a couple of tablespoons of sugar, pour on a jigger of rum, and light. Serve at once.

"Then pour more rum, the
bottles stopping,
Stir it again and say it's topping."
OLD NEW ENGLAND RHYME

Peach Filbert Fritters

Peel 4 ripe peaches and cut them in eighths, then dip in strained raspberry jam. Roll quickly in finely chopped filberts, then dip in beaten egg and then in crumbs. Work quickly. Chill well until dessert time, then cook carefully in ¼ cup of butter, first on one side, then on the other. Serve hot, with a shaker of powdered sugar. These may be flamed with brandy or rum but the procedure is superfluous.

"Blooming ambrosial fruit of vegetable gold."

JOHN MILTON

Fried Pears with Chocolate Sauce

And I am the first to admit that *that* sounds awful! Peel halves of 3 ripe Bartlett pears and remove cores. Fry in the blazer in ¼ cup of butter until a light gold on both sides. Sprinkle with a little granulated sugar, pour on ¼ cup of rum, and light. Serve when the flames die down, with a thin chocolate sauce. Or skip the chocolate and serve sprinkled with toasted almonds and accompanied by sour cream. That's a better idea.

"And damn'd be he that first cries, 'Hold, enough!'"

W. SHAKESPEARE

Rummed Pineapple

Peel half a ripe pineapple and cut in finger-sized pieces (or use canned pineapple). In the blazer melt ⅛ pound of butter and sauté the slices until lightly browned on both sides. Sprinkle the pineapple with 2 tablespoons of granulated sugar, add 2 jiggers of rum, and cook until the rum is almost absorbed, then pour in ¾ cup of heavy cream. As soon as the cream is hot, serve with lady-fingers.

"Pineapple is great—she is indeed almost too transcendent a delight, if not sinful, yet so like sinning that really a tender-conscienced person would do well to pause."

CHARLES LAMB

Prune Fritters

Soak ½ pound of jumbo prunes in a cup of sherry for 5 or 6 hours. Drain and remove pits, and replace with pieces of walnut meats, then flatten them slightly. Make a fritter batter (2 eggs, ⅔ cup of milk, 1 cup of flour, ½ teaspoon of salt, 1 tablespoon of melted butter). Now melt ½ pound of butter in the blazer, and when it is hot, bubbling hot, dip the prunes into the fritter batter and then place in the hot butter. As they brown on one side, turn them to brown on the other. Drain them with a slotted spoon and serve with a shaker of powdered sugar and a wedge of lemon—or with a rum sauce. So you don't like prunes?

Rum Sauce: Heat in blazer ¼ pound of butter, 1 cup of XXXX sugar, 1 egg, and 3 tablespoons of Jamaica rum, beating until hot and foamy.

Strawberry or Jam Toasts

This is a neat way of turning stale cake and jam into a glamorous dessert. Dip slices of stale sponge, angel, or pound cake in a mixture of ½ cup of milk beaten with an egg. Sauté in butter until golden on both sides. Put a spoonful of strawberry, apricot, or other jam on each piece, drizzle with a little brandy or rum, and heat another minute before serving with cold sour or whipped cream.

"The table is the only place where we do not get weary the first hour."

BRILLAT-SAVARIN

138

Flaming Strawberries with Orange

Cut the zest—the very outer orange skin of the orange—into pin-sized pieces, and cook them in the blazer with a cup of orange juice and ¼ cup of sugar for 3 or 4 minutes. Add 3 cups of whole hulled strawberries, turn for a minute in the syrup, pour in 3 jiggers of brandy and light. Serve, flaming, with vanilla ice cream or with very well chilled whipped cream. Any fruit may be poached in this syrup and served in this manner.

*"Know'st thou the land where the lemon
      trees bloom,
Where the gold orange glows in the
      deep thickets gloom?"*
                    JOHANN VON GOETHE

Zabaglione

Beat 7 egg yolks until thick with ½ cup of sugar. Meantime beat ½ cup of Marsala (or a sweet, heavy-bodied sherry) in the blazer. (The old Italian way of measuring the Marsala is ½ eggshell full of Marsala for every egg yolk, but this is alarmingly inaccurate, as the amount varies from less than 1 tablespoon to more than 2!) Add the beaten egg mixture to the hot Marsala, put over hot water jacket, and beat with a whisk until thick, hot, and creamy. (Watch it! As in the following recipe, overcooking will curdle it.) Serve hot in glasses. Rum may be used, in smaller amounts, in place of the Marsala.

> *"We'll dine and drink, and say if we think*
> *That anything better can be;*
> *And when we have dined, wish all*
> *mankind*
> *May dine as well as we."*
>
> THOMAS LOVE PEACOCK

140

Coffee-Rum Zabaglione

Make ½ pint of triple-strength coffee (¼ cup of coffee to 8 ounces of boiling water), put it in the blazer over the hot water jacket, add 7 egg yolks beaten very light with ½ cup of fine granulated sugar and a jigger of rum, and beat constantly with a whip until it has thickened. (Do not overcook or it will curdle!) Serve at once in individual glasses, and accompany with thin rich cookies.

"O, boiling bubbling berry bean:
Thou consort of the kitchen Queen—
Browned and ground of every feature
The only aromatic creature,
For which we long!"

ARTHUR GRAY

Café Diable

Put a quart of triple-strength coffee into the blazer, add 15 whole cloves, a long stick of cinnamon, the rind of an orange cut in a long continuous spiral, and 10 lumps of sugar. Heat this well, then add ½ cup of Cognac. Pour another ¼ cup of Cognac in a ladle, warm and light it, then pour it over the coffee and allow it to burn before serving.

"Sinament and ginger,
Nutmeg and cloves
And they gave me
This jolly red nose."
BEAUMONT & FLETCHER

Index

Index